One Language

One Language
Anastasia Taylor-Lind

smith|doorstop

the poetry business

Published 2022 by The Poetry Business
Campo House,
54 Campo Lane,
Sheffield S1 2EG
www.poetrybusiness.co.uk

Copyright © Anastasia Taylor-Lind 2022
The moral rights of the author have been asserted.
ISBN 978-1-914914-10-2
eBook ISBN 978-1-914914-11-9

All rights reserved.
Without limiting the rights under copyright reserved above,
no part of this publication may be reproduced, stored in or introduced
into a retrieval system, or transmitted, in any form or by any means
(electronic, mechanical, photocopying, recording or otherwise),
without the prior written permission of both the copyright owner
and the above publisher of this book.

Designed & typeset by The Poetry Business.
Printed by Imprint Digital.

British Library Cataloguing-in-Publication Data.
A catalogue record for this book is available from the British Library.

Smith|Doorstop is a member of Inpress
www.inpressbooks.co.uk.
Distributed by IPS UK, 1 Deltic Avenue,
Rooksley, Milton Keynes MK13 8LD.

The Poetry Business gratefully acknowledges the support
of Arts Council England.

For my heroic and brilliant Mum

Contents

11	Rewind
13	1st Nat Geo Assignment
14	Editing
15	Field Notes
	October 27th 2020, 7am
	09.05
	11.36
	14.15
	16.00
	16.57
	17.21
	17.45
	18.10
	22.30
33	Stories
	Ajdabiya
	Al Hikma Hospital
	Welcome to Donetsk
	In a town recently re-taken by the army
	Translating Cause of Death
	Shooting
45	Stories No One Wants To Hear
	i–xii
61	Spring 1941
62	Spring 2011
63	Acknowledgements
64	Captions

Rewind

It's 9/11 the first time you stay.
In the morning you bring Taliban poems back to bed.
I drink cardamom coffee and you read their tender lines
'May you not be hungry in the desert, my dear'.
Their loving as ordinary as ours.

I see wilding men shouldering RPGs by the swimming pool
of a warlord's compound and think they're beautiful,
watch a dentist fall to Earth from an aeroplane undercarriage
rising over Kabul.
Human payload slipping from the landing gear,
falling through swipes, scrolls and clicks.
Rewind the tapes, see the little man flying upwards,
returning to his life,
rewind the tapes.

Like Bruegel's Icarus, he touches down with a splash
in a rooftop water tank 4km away,
his suffering unnoticed
except for a casual cell phone recording.

Twenty years ago, the twin towers man fell too,
twisting and turning, tie fluttering,
past flames and smoke, for a moment head first over Manhattan.
Rewind the tapes, see the little men flying upwards,
returning to their lives,
rewind the tapes.

We lie under a marigold-embroidered bedspread
bought in Afghanistan.
I'm afraid of you,
not you exactly, but of falling for you.

My old friend Tom took me on that shopping trip
in an armoured vehicle with his bodyguard
and I remembered the summer before the end of uni,
how he and I sat up late, drinking Jameson,
listening to Johnny Cash
and imagining our own deaths,
together, somewhere in a dusty alley,
all golden light, slow motion and elevated camera angles.
We took it in turns who was doing the dying
and who was doing the cradling.

1st Nat Geo Assignment

Where the rivers meet, I watch two policemen
prod a baby with sticks,
its plump white body bobbing face down in the cold water,
swimmers crawling past a few metres away.

Another woman looks on from the flood barrier
with crossed arms.
Probably a girl, she says as the men continue to fish,
downstream of the largest concrete structure on earth.

Editing

An October morning before a grey soft-box dawn.
Sit at the computer, coffee, cigarette.

Flip steadily through ten thousand frames until
you find yourself reflected in a woman's eyes,

your figure caught in the catch-light of her cornea.
There she is – pastel pink *shalwar kameez*,
one fly resting on the embroidered trim.

After walking for eight days to reach the border
here she is, looking up into your white face.

Field Notes

Nagorno-Karabakh

*October 27th 2020, 7am –
meet Kristen at Heathrow Terminal 2,
flight AF1681 to Yerevan, via Paris.*

*10,311 dollars in cash, 2 cameras, 150 rolls of Fuji film,
20 notebooks, Armenian press card application,
Nagorno-Karabakh visa application,
x 2, all printed.*

*40kg excess baggage; 4 bulletproof vests, 4 ballistics helmets,
3 battlefield med kits, 2 sleeping bags, 8 sets of full PPE,
several hundred facemasks.*

09.05

The hair salons in Stepanakert closed in late September –
women's roots are as long as the war, a grey inch for each month.

This morning men gather at the government building
around a large military map that falls over the edges

of a desk belonging to the director of Emergency Situations.
They look for their missing sons. It's my job to photograph this.

One Father finds his on Telegram, pixelated and de-faced.
At the morgue, unrecognisable remains wait on DNA matches.

Soldiers sing to their mothers on YouTube
and cry for them from hospital beds.

This is the first war to start during the pandemic. Mostly, we're the only journalists wearing facemasks and the only all-female reporting team – after a few weeks, we hear people referring to us as 'the girls from Nat Geo'.

Others mask-shame us. A French photographer walks up to me at the hospital – 'Why are you wearing a mask? There's no Covid here.' There is and we're reporting on it. Back at the hotel, a Russian journalist asks 'How am I gonna kiss you on the lips when you're wearing that mask?'

*How to tell a war story in pictures –
always photograph wounded soldiers, frightened civilians,
mourning relatives, the aftermath of shelling, food queues,
the bus station, daily life continuing as normal. Wait outside
the emergency department for casualties, look for fresh graves
at the cemetery, drive to the frontline and see what happens.*

11.36

Khanum takes her fur coat, uproots two rose bushes
from the garden, packs them in waterlogged soil.
Her husband wraps the best plates in old newspaper,

throws a pregnant dog in the truck. There's no room
for last year's pickles. They don't torch their house
like everyone else, although I hope they will.

14.15

The frescos at Dadivank are cut down, stone Khachkars
removed from their enclaves. A priest shouts *No fotos, no fotos!*

but the Ministry of Foreign Affairs has bussed in journalists.
Evacuating the monastery is something they want us to see.

Babushkas light candles while Instagram influencers weep
in their selfies and Russian peacekeepers pose
like cellphone celebrities.

*A house in the valley below goes up in flames. Is it a
coincidence this happens when the bus of foreign journalists
arrives – could it be planned? I feel bad for thinking this.*

*People are suffering and they know how their suffering looks in
pictures. I don't photograph anything that's staged for the press
but I can't always tell what is real and what's not.*

16.00

In Kalbajar, all valuables are taken. A narrow newly dug ditch
follows the curve of road – water pipes.

Engineers dismantle turbines at the hydroelectric plant,
the school roof is gone. What is left is burned.

> *On the northern road to Armenia, the only route out of
> Karabakh, I need a piss. We stop at a chalet-style hotel near
> the hot springs. I get out in an empty car park, follow the
> bathroom signs down steps behind the building. The toilet has
> already been dismantled, there's just a plumbing pipe left in
> the concrete floor, too small for my aim.*

I was here before, in 2011, when Ivor and I were still together. I had just turned 30 and was thinking a lot about having kids. Now I'm 40 and thinking a lot about not having them. Ivor doesn't talk to me anymore. Mum says he's covering the Azerbaijani side of the war for The New York Times. *I dream about him every night. It stops when I go home.*

16.57

At a mountaintop cemetery, someone unearths the bodies
of their grandparents and packs them too.

Smoke haze, warm light, chill air and end of summer grass.
Rusted railings on the burial plot have been prised open.

A coffin-shaped outline remains at the bottom of an empty hole,
the black satin lining hasn't rotted yet.

17.21

We walk across the street to an empty room
where the police chief toasts to *Game Over*.

He invites us to drink homemade vodka
poured from a Coca Cola bottle,
to eat canned fish and bread – a long-life last supper.

*We brought our friend home from the frontline
in a carrier bag* he says.

> Security evaluation – Kristen and I are alone.
> This is a group of men with guns. Men with guns are
> dangerous. Drunk men with guns are even more dangerous.
> I feel bad for thinking this.
>
> Nothing happened – if it did I'd edit out these men
> as if they never existed.
>
> Hollywood directors like their female journalists
> to seduce the people they report on.
> My male colleagues talk about the specific thrill
> of fucking-under-fire.

17.45

We stalk through the valley looking for more stories,
no one's in the mood to talk.

There's a 4x4 outside almost every home – reporters!
This one's already taken, then the next and another.

When buildings burn from the inside they look like gingerbread
houses with embered eaves instead of icing sugar.

We've run out of money. It's easy to burn through money in a war zone – public transport is suspended, drivers are hard to find, drivers with good cars even harder. Prices go up. Only expensive hotels are safe – occupied by foreigners they're less likely targets, we hope. Expensive hotels are also easily identifiable on a map and less likely hit by mistake, we hope.

Always a translator shortage when the foreign press arrives. Prices go up. Supply routes are disrupted, food becomes scarce, prices go up. I call my editor in America – she promises to pay our expenses whatever we come back with but it's her word and no contract.

18.10

Our tyre blows at dusk on a dirt road and Zory changes it.
Chainsaws murmur and woodcutter's flashlights
are constellations of fireflies on the dark hillside
as Armenians loot the land for winter wood.

> *It's batshit crazy they would rather destroy everything*
> *than leave it for their enemy.*
> *I feel bad for thinking this.*
>
> *Zory – a childhood friend of our translator is jittery, battle*
> *fatigued and slogs through a pocket-sized bottle of brandy 'to*
> *keep warm'. It's our first day working together –*
> *he drives too fast.*
>
> *Car crashes are the biggest killer of journalists in the field.*
> *I tell this to everyone I work with.*

22.30

We pass trucks later on the way out, ditching logs by the side
of the road – their load too heavy to make it over the pass.

A trail of headlights mapping miles of mountain contours
towards the border, grey exhaust fumes rising
into the cold night air.

It's a mess. The handover is at midnight
and the world ends in a traffic jam.

It's too dark to make pictures.

Stories

Ajdabiya

I don't remember your name.
I left it in Ivor's notebook
translated from phonetic Arabic
next to details of the assault on Brega.

I didn't find your family
and I didn't show them your photograph.
I didn't even print it.

I remember your profile sharply illuminated
by the surgical spotlight suspended
above your closed eyes.
I remember the journo excuses –
the bright light
we were shining
on a dark corner of the world.

I remember the editor who said people only care
about places they've been on holiday.
And advertisers won't buy page space next to the dead.

I can still see the padded bandage
that held your head
and hid the bullet hole.
Blood seeping through the gauze
at the nape of your neck.
A trickle coagulated on your ear.
The smell of a butcher's block on a hot day.

I remember struggling with the exposure,
metering for your face
and eliminating the emergency room with my aperture.

The relentless clicking of our cameras
and the moaning of the legless man
on the gurney next to you.
Sniper the doctor said.

Yes, I remember you. The first man I watched die.
But I don't remember your name.

Al Hikma Hospital

A cameraman walks towards a patient lying under a blue sheet on the operating table. Two pairs of gloved and bloodied hands move over an open stomach. Beeping of medical machines. An overwhelming array of surgical instruments line up between the patient's legs. A headline appears on the screen in English GEY MARTHON – BRITISH (PRESS).

The camera zooms in on bloodied hands stitching something together in a big red hole. Spotlights burn a white circle obscuring the abdomen but I think I can make out intestines. Other pieces of insides are clipped together with metal forceps around the edges. He is unconscious, bare arms falling off the table and head tilted back, a tube protruding from his mouth. His face is deeply tanned and unshaven from months in the desert, and looks so unharmed it is hard to believe it belongs to this body and to my friend Guy Martin.

CUT

Chris Hondros unconscious on a blood-splattered bed. Eyes closed, purple face, thickly bandaged head. Someone pumps breath into lungs with a manual respirator while a pair of hands scissor his shirt.

CUT

Tim Hetherington, dead on a gurney. A man softly eases each eyelid down with thumb and index finger. Tim's bare feet are tied together with white cotton at the ankles and big toes. Another man binds his jaw closed. Someone else, in civilian clothes, makes a picture of Tim's face with a compact camera.

Welcome to Donetsk

You teach me this wartime trick –
to look for living pot plants
in the windows on Kievska Avenue.
Most are crisped and brown.

But one green geranium
and a succulent spider plant
offer proof of life
for the person who waters them.

Whole apartment blocks are abandoned.
Collapsed telephone lines,
blown-up branches
litter the road.

No voices,
no tinkering metalwork in the distance,
no buses, no playing children.
Leaves rustle white noise.

You say *It's like Sunday, every day.*
Stray dogs and swallows,
and the soft thud of shelling.

In a town recently re-taken by the Army I buy a postcard of Donetsk on a summer evening. Rose bushes fill the foreground. A couple arm in arm on a paved promenade gaze out over a river, like shepherds on the hillside of a painting.

It's picture postcard perfect. Photoshopped. Probably staged. Here, Donetsk looks like my home town. No combatants, no soldiers, no separatists, no rebels, no terrorists, no volunteers, no protestors, no refugees, no collateral damage, no civilian casualties.

In newspaper photographs Donetsk resembles Grozny in the nineties. There, war is only checkpoints, flags on the town hall, men in mismatched combat fatigues, empty supermarkets, curfews and families fractured by the frontline. Smashed dinner sets, blown-out windows, shrapnel in the vegetable patch, closed banks, cash under the bed and cars filled with belongings.

Translating Cause of Death

Shelling near the house. Shelling on the street. Shelling in the backyard. Killed by shelling while fishing on his birthday. During shelling was torn into pieces. Mortar arrived in her bedroom. Direct hit of a shell to the house. Mortar shelling on the city market. Killed in her garden by shrapnel, buried in the same place. Shelling, 10-months old. Shelling, was on the bus. Shelling, one month old. Grad hit where boys were playing. Shelling. Shelling. Priest. Came from Kiev to visit his mother, stepped on a mine. Shelling. Bus driver, shelling. Car exploded on road between two towns. Shot by rebels on the street for breaking curfew. Shelling. Scientist, academic, university teacher. Shelling on the market. Shelling, it was his birthday. Shelling. Was shot by rebels on the way to church. Shelling. Didn't stop at the checkpoint. Shelling. Was driving his cattle trailer. Shelling. Went to the shop with her mother. Shell hit her house and she burned alive. Mother and daughter. Bus driver. Priest. Doctor, surgeon. Ambulance driver. School teacher. Mortar. Engineer at coke plant coming home from work.

Shooting

What have you been shooting?
an editor asks one afternoon
in the South of France – table service,
Aperol spritz, sunglasses and sunshine.

We say we shoot people,
fire shutters, take pictures,
capture subjects with cameras
and expose them onto film.
Warfare's words ingrained in our lexicon.

*

The Comanche married guns
and horses on the great planes –
combining speed and fire power
changed the battlefield forever.

Cameras, again.
I wonder what shutter-speed
Capa shot the falling soldier with –
perhaps a 125th of a second.
Fast enough to capture
the moment of death
for the first time.

*

One afternoon another year,
under a sunless grey sky
Berehynia looks out from her pedestal
on the Black Square. Men stretcher
the wounded down a hill
leaving a trail of bright red arterial blood
across the cobblestones, fresh and thick.

I follow,
picking my way
through smouldering debris
and broken glass,
my face covered with soot
from burning tyres;
a *Maidan-tan*.

Corpses lie under a barricade,
each tucked in with a blanket.
Grey and waxy faces, blue lips,
each with a single bullet hole
to the forehead, or chest.

Each ready for his close up;
I shoot them like everybody else.
Under a hot shower at night
the water runs black over my feet.

Stories No One Wants To Hear

i.

Alcoholics don't dream is not a metaphor

I invite Dad to dinner
since he's dead he can show up any time

he arrives at 36 when he became my father
and the age I was when he died

I play the Dad's dead mix-tape my brother made
for our drive to his funeral

we sing Cat Stevens's 'Where Do The Children Play?'
and smoke roll-ups out the back door

ii.

what's for dinner?

a childhood game for when he fed me
from empty end-of-week cupboards
before the trip to town and Giro

what do you want Dad replies
fresh pineapples, whole coconuts,
a bushel of yellow dates?

I play along; *tinned peaches,*
meringue nests, toasted tea
cakes and penny sweets

tonight my kitchen shelves are crammed
I lay the table and we slather Camembert
onto a French stick, spoon ripe avocados,

pluck sun dried tomatoes from the fatty brine
lick orange oil from our fingers and thumbs
no one drinks, no hands tremor

iii.

in a corner of the field where I grew up
blackberry briars built a wall
of thorns around Dad's grave

lilac wrapped limbs
around the caravan door, moss crept
over piles of empty wine bottles

using Dad's old tools, my brother and I
dug his grave after watching a YouTube video
on how to dig a grave

we pitched spade through root,
clumps of clay
my palms bled the deeper we got

the harder to stay in the hole,
one swinging pick axe, the other a shovel,
back to back until we hit the water table

iv.

On the way home from the pub, Dad, Brother and I stop at the top of Pinkworthy Hill, at the bend in the road where we saw fireflies once, for a pissing competition. A race to see whose stream runs furthest down the Devon lane. Dad wins – our halfs of lemonade no match for his four pints of lager.

The caravan has no plumbing. On cold nights, Dad and Brother piss out the door into a bucket. Me too, one un-pyjamad leg swinging out, cocked over the rim, bracing myself off the aluminium frame, my aim inferior.

I'd practice peeing like a horse too, naked and barefoot in the field on tip-toes, bandy legs, back arched, releasing into the long spring grass, piss trickling down the insides of my thighs.

In Libya the threat of unexploded ordinance makes the verge a no-mans-land for pissers. Squatting to expose my fleshy white backside, I feel the warm spray of splashback on my ankles, ricocheting off hot tarmac with velocity after holding it in for hours. Incoming, fright and flight, hobbled by the jeans that knot my feet together.

Winter in Ukraine and hay-sweet steam rising between my haunches, warmth reaching my nostrils, an amber pool of urine thawing frosted grass. Shaken hips, damp knickers, drip drying.

In Uganda they say *Do you want stop and check the tyres?* Too polite to ask the real question.

v.

Isn't it dangerous to be a woman? Surrounded by men, questions about risk-taking, parenting (I'm childless) and personal relationships are directed at me. I am a female photojournalist, Guy is a photojournalist, and Ivor's male gaze is just his own.

Has anyone ever hurt you? is what they are really asking. They have but not in the field. War, depending on how you define it, is everywhere and home is the place where women and girls face the greatest threat of violence. It is safe here, but not out there, has been used to confine us for centuries.

My dad beat my mum, and me too when I tried to protect her. We all seek to reproduce the familiar conditions of our childhood, even when we are trying to escape them. Violence is familiar to me, it has always been present in my life and my relationship with it shaped my relationship with photography.

I was less than a year old when I first watched a punch-up, from my mum's arms and at a safe distance, according to her. We were at a Gypsy horse fair in Suffolk when around a hundred people beat each other in a beer tent over a trotting horse crash. *Thank God you were too young to remember*, Mum said, and I was, because this was the first I'd heard of it.

vi.

My dad had been a teenage boxer in the East End, like his dad. It was him who taught me how to throw a punch, the summer before starting high school, coaching me through little techniques – making impact while my arm was still tightly into my chest and keeping my weight centred. Tivvy High was rough and he encouraged me to hit anyone who bullied me. He said *Anastasia, some people only understand one language.*

My dad was the first person I punched, to stop him from hitting my mum.

vii.

I called the police for the first time at the end of July or beginning of August 1993.

B.T had thrown plates at me and tried to strangle me. I went to my caravan, then he repeatedly banged hard at the window and walls and shouted abuse, both I and the children were extremely frightened.

I phoned the police, who came (one man and one woman). They asked B.T to stay in his caravan and me in mine, for the rest of the night, which we did.

Second time B.T called the police. He had continued with his attacks on me through the month of August by hitting me, and trying to strangle me, I had bruises on my face and neck, he had cut my telephone line and smashed a kitchen cabinet and wooden chest with an axe.

B.T was also at this time violent to Anastasia. It wasn't till the autumn of 1994 that I took her to the doctor (Dr Saville, Tiverton).

viii.

I do remember this. Being taken there, not for treatment, but to record the marks on my arms and legs after an attack. A humiliating, clinical and methodical process. The doctor made notes on the length and position of scratches. Maybe he photographed them. I kept a straight face. If I acted like everything was OK, it would be. Polite. Process. Paperwork. The bureaucracy of violence.

I read these custody transcripts for the first time. Mum and I talk it through. She tells me about a time we were leaving for a party when Dad gave her a black eye.

Did we go to the party?

Yes.

What, with a black eye? is all I say.

ix.

The second person I hit was Laura Packer for calling my pony Melody ugly. We were twelve and I knocked out one of her front teeth at lunchtime. At my school arguments were settled when one party officially challenged the other to a scrap at a designated time. Word spread through classrooms and later a crowd gathered to watch the duel until some teacher heard the jeering and broke it up. I hated school and got in trouble often.

The third person I punched was Philippa Cottrell, in maths class a few years later. She was one of the toughest bullies and I wasn't quiet enough to go unnoticed. Telling the teachers didn't stop Philippa. On this day there was a faint-hearted supply teacher standing in. The classroom belonged to Philippa. From her elite position on the back row she used a ruler to pelt the back of my head with chewed up jotter paper. I sat in humiliating silence for a few minutes, knowing the supply teacher would not do anything.

I found myself folded over Philippa, the fingers of one hand tangled in her thick curly fringe, while I pummelled her in the face with the other. I got two punches in before Claire Agnew pulled me off and the supply teacher went running for help.

I'd only bloodied Philippa's nose, but I'd done it in front of everyone and I was never picked on again.

x.

The first time I encountered violence as a photographer was on my 21st birthday.

I was making pictures for university at a Gypsy fair in Stowe-on-the-Wold and Dad's old friend Mark Palmer took me for drinks that evening. An altercation began between two men – each of them standing, chests puffed, removing their coats with ceremony. I realised too late that I was the only woman left in the pub and then the whole room went at each other with fists, beer glasses and chairs.

Mark climbed onto his seat to get a better view and calmly reviewed the chaos with crossed arms, while the men next to us pushed me and a young boy under the table, covering us with their coats. Shaking and with my arms around the boy, I told him *Don't worry, it'll be ok.*

I know. It's always like this he said. I stuck my head out once during the fight and saw, through the window, a group of men pulling down a lamppost and using it as a battering ram against the door. Beyond them stood a line of police – silent and still. Mark told me to get out and make pictures. I didn't. I was too afraid.

Witnessing violence played out on many different scales led me to become a pacifist, to oppose violent solutions under any circumstances – personal or political. Sure I would never hit anyone again.

xi.

A cold December evening in a South London pub with a big photo crowd after an exhibition opening.

A few months earlier my friend Guy had been blown up and though now recovering would be disabled for life. A bald, thick-set photojournalist in his late thirties came up to me, drunk and looking for confrontation. He insulted Guy. The whole pub went silent, watching.

I tried ignoring him but he just got louder, nastier. Pride and loyalty wouldn't let me leave the room. When I tried to speak he shouted over me that we all know Guy made money from getting injured.

I remember hearing that. Then I was staring into his eyes, hitting him with a left, then a right, then Ivor was dragging me away.

Two bystanders hoisted the man up. He was shouting *You're fucked in the head, Anastasia, fucked in the head. You've got fucking PTSD.*

xii.

I should not have hit him. The illogic of violence only made sense in that moment of utter frustration when I was unable to reach this man with words.

Anastasia, some people only understand one language.

And if I ask myself now – given the chance, would I have shot the Libyan soldier who trained the mortar onto Guy and his friends on Tripoli Street, in order to stop him from firing that lethal round, the answer is *yes*. And there it is – the system and the structure and the indoctrination of the war machine that drives people to kill in the defence of the man next to him, not his country and not his ideology but in defence of his friend.

Pacifism is a privilege of the peaceful and empowered – inside the home, in our communities and on a global scale. For the most part I own those privileges but when I don't it's harder to be a pacifist.

I've tried to tell these stories in professional discussions about violence so many times but no one wants to hear them.

Spring 1941

A full-length formal portrait, regimented, almost ethnographic. Alfie stands *at ease*, legs wide, hands clasped behind his back. Being photographed is taken seriously. Deep set eyes, furrowed brow, squinting into the sun wearing desert issue khaki, high-waisted shorts, wool socks to the knee.

His top button is undone, the collar folded flat along slight shoulders, sleeves rolled up unevenly. The straight horizon cutting through his biceps reveals imbalance in the folded fabric. I am looking for things that mark him apart, something that makes him ours. Maybe it is in the sleeves.

Alfie was afraid of the dark. When they were kids, Nan took him to the outhouse at night because he was too scared to go alone. He wrote from Tobruk on night duty to tell her he wasn't afraid anymore. Alfie died in the breakout of the city and was buried there. No one ever visited his grave. My dad was named after him.

Spring 2011

I spent my first night in Libya in Tobruk, at the Al Masira Hotel, newly built and almost deserted because of the war. Food shortages had closed the kitchen – biscuits and orange squash for dinner.

The next day I drove West to Benghazi and to the shifting frontline in the desert along the Via Balbia highway. This patch of coastal road had been fought over in 1941, the year Alfie died.

Died, as Allied forces tried to halt the Nazi advance from Tripoli. The road was again of strategic importance, as Gaddafi's army moved eastwards making contact with the rebels.

That morning I had found Alfie's grave in the Commonwealth War Cemetery, an imperial, landscaped garden with immaculately kept rows of headstones. Plot number 8.E.6.

He is buried in bare, dry earth close to the perimeter wall, beside agricultural fields and grazing camels. Small and delicate flowers grow as weeds, yellow and purple, on his grave. I picked a bunch and left them there.

I also pressed some in my notebook and posted them to Nan in a plastic 35mm film canister.

Acknowledgements

With immense gratitude to the people, and especially the strong women, who invite me into their homes and lives and share their stories with me.

Thank you to the beautiful and generous writers have who have accompanied me on my poetry journey – my teachers Rachael Allen, Daljit Nagra, Richard Scott, Maurice Riordan and Rachel Long. Dear writer friends Jennifer Nadel, Alisa Sopova, Adrian Nicole LeBlanc, MT Connolly, Alim Remtulla, Joanne Drayton, Anne Bernays, Olivier Laurent, Kristen Chick, Camilla Naprous and Garnette Cadogan. The editor of this collection, Ann Sansom, and also Katie McLean at Smith|Doorstop.

The Nieman Fellowship at Harvard, The Carey Institute for Global Good and The London Library Emerging Writers Programme for gifting me invaluable time and support to develop my writing.

Thank you to my brother for sharing a love of poetry and always being my first reader. And to Dad – I'm grateful for everything you taught me.

Captions

Cover
: Evacuation of Dadivank Monastery, Kalbajar district, Nagorno-Karabakh (November 2020).

Inside Cover (front)
: Female teams conduct door-to-door polio vaccinations in Jalalabad, Afghanistan (August 2013).

23 Arina and Angelina Hakobyan in bed, Kolatak village, Nagorno-Karabakh (November 2020).

24 Lunch table at the Hakobyan family home in Kolatak village, Nagorno-Karabakh (November 2020).

31 Car damaged by shelling in central Stepanakert, Nagorno-Karabakh (November 2020).

32 Freshly dug grave at the military graveyard in Stepanakert, Nagorno-Karabakh (November 2020).

43 A Ukrainian soldier at a position near Peski, Donetsk, Eastern Ukraine (July 2018).

44 Postcard of Donetsk before the war, Eastern Ukraine (Image © Kohanovsky).

59 Me and Dad with horses, Star and Blue, and the wagon (Photograph by Mum, 1983).

60 Portrait of my great uncle, Alfie Taylor, during World War II.

Inside Cover (back)
: Rebel forces on the Via Balbia highway near Ajdabiya, Libya (April 2011).